IS GOD REAL
AND DOES IT EVEN MATTER?

IS GOD REAL
AND DOES IT EVEN MATTER?

RICK FURMANEK

Light Chaser Press
www.lightchaserpress.com

IS GOD REAL AND DOES IT EVEN MATTER?
Copyright ©2017 Rick Furmanek

Published by Light Chaser Press
PO Box 2194, Gilbert, Arizona 85299
www.lightchaserpress.com

All rights reserved. No part of this publication may be reproduced, stored in a retrieval system or transmitted in any form by any means, electronic, mechanical, digital, photocopy, recording, or any other without the prior written permission of the publisher. The only exception is brief quotations in printed and electronic reviews.

Scripture quotations are from the ESV® Bible (The Holy Bible, English Standard Version®), copyright ©2001 by Crossway, a publishing ministry of Good News Publishers. Used by permission. All rights reserved.

Scripture quotations are taken from the Holy Bible, New Living Translation, copyright ©1996, 2004, 2007, 2013, 2015 by Tyndale House Foundation. Used by permission of Tyndale House Publishers, Inc., Carol Stream, Illinois 60188. All rights reserved.

Italics indicate emphasis added.

Library of Congress Control Number 2017909786

ISBN 978-09883499-2-6

First printing, 2017
Also available in eBook

Printed in the United States of America

To my beautiful wife, Robin, who has faithfully walked beside me every single step of my journey.

To my sweet daughter-in-law, Savanna, who has made God the most important thing in her life.

To my wonderful mother, Belva, who continues to amaze me with her desire to know more of Jesus.

Table of Contents

Introduction	9
1. Perception vs. Reality	13
2. Not Just Any God	21
3. Only One God	27
4. What It Means to Believe in God	40
5. Why the World Doesn't Believe	46
6. Why We Don't Believe	51
7. Understanding What is at Stake	58
8. The Solution to Our Dilemma	63
9. The Recipe for Relationship	67
10. The First Ingredient: Conviction	70
11. The Second Ingredient: Confession	75
12. The Third Ingredient: Reconciliation	79
13. The Fourth Ingredient: Redirection	103
14. I Once Was Blind but Now I See	116
15. What Now?	124
16. It's Your Move	129
Final Thoughts	134

Introduction

It would be interesting to know what prompted you initially to pick up this book.

For some, your intent may be to only provide a *courtesy read*. It could be that a friend or a family member—someone you respect—asked you to look it over and give it some consideration.

For others, you are embarking on this as a *curious read*. You might be one who enjoys the opportunity to learn another's perspective on the origins of good vs. evil. You find it intriguing to ponder life and death matters, and the challenging notion that there could be an eternity to be experienced.

Still, for others, your aim is to give this book a *critical read*. You perhaps have already made up your mind regarding the only one God vs. the gods of other world religions vs. no god debate; supernatural creation vs. naturalistic evolution; the necessity of faith vs. no faith needed; and the issue of moral accountability vs. no moral accountability. Thus, your objective is to familiarize yourself with this material in an effort to reinforce your own position.

And still again, for others, you are expecting this exercise to be somewhat of a *cynical read*. Your own personal story is filled with countless accounts of betrayal, desperation and disappointment, which have led you to the conclusion that it is altogether unrealistic to accept with any credible certainty that there is a God who would actually care about you. Disillusioned with the prospect that life could possess any real significant purpose, you now find yourself in a place where you hesitate to trust anyone who would seek to convince you otherwise. Yet, in spite of feeling like this, there remains an inexplicable yearning within to continue canvassing the possibility that your life could be different.

Whatever your motivation for reading, please consider the subject matter very carefully. There has been a specific prayer offered on your behalf, that as you close the final page you will begin to see things differently; that you will want to become fully engaged with the truth of this message; and thus, experience the supernatural transformation—as countless others have—that is available to you through the power of the One who stands behind this message. The premise of the book is this: The existence of God is much more than just a matter of one's own personal opinion. How a person chooses to believe or not believe will govern his or her manner of living in the present and will set the course for their eternity.

> "The thief comes only to steal and kill and destroy. I came that they may have life and have it abundantly."
>
> John 10:10

> "And this is the promise that he made to us—eternal life."
>
> 1 John 2:25

Is God Real and Does It Even Matter?

1.
Perception vs. Reality

Do any of these questions sound familiar?

• While the advancements in science and technology are accomplishing so much good, why is our behavior toward one another getting worse?
• Why is honesty rarely celebrated anymore while dishonesty can get a person both fame and promotion?
• Why does wealth come so easily to some people while others who work as hard or harder always struggle to make ends meet?
• Why are some people free of addictions — even the temptation — while others always seem to be living in some sort of bondage?
• Why do bad things continue to happen to the good people I know?
• Why do innocent people die before their time?

When we begin to verbalize the *'Why?'* questions of life, more often than not it is a reflection of a more basic question, *"Why me?"* When life gets difficult, when unforeseen adversity throws us off course and calamity and/or chaos ensues, our inclination is to take on an apathetic, sarcastic, or even a destructive attitude toward our existence and the purpose of life itself.

To counter this impulse, one must be willing to consider these questions in a completely different light. To begin, take a moment and reread each question carefully and see if you can pick up on the universal thread that runs through each one.

Did you reread them? Did you pick up on a common expression? Here it is. These six commonly asked questions depict events and/or circumstances that reside outside of *our ability to control.*

And what makes our run-amuck situation seem even more desperate are the enticing commercials and infomercials out there assuring us that we deserve good health, financial freedom, ease of life, and a secure retirement... and that if we'll just follow a few easy steps, our dreams and aspirations will all come true.

Let's be realistic; a few simple observations during a normal day will reveal that we do not have the ability to control what goes on in life to the level we often are led to believe we have. Consider some of the most basic details of life itself; we have no say to whom, where, and when we will be born; what color our eyes will be, the color of our skin, or when our hair, or lack thereof, will begin revealing our age. We have no say when a stranger will choose to show us kindness, or when someone will decide to do us harm. Finally, we do not have say over when our own life will come to an end. All one need do is consider the countless accounts describing people who attempted to take their own life, or were told they would die within a certain time frame by a medical professional, but miraculously lived on, as well as those who made every effort to extend their life... yet died.

The concept of life and who ultimately controls it is really not a new conversation. It's just that today a wider range of personalities are competing for your loyalty; determined to persuade you — and your bank account — that they alone hold the necessary tools that can empower you to control your life now as well as your future.

In light of all the contradictory promises swirling around us, this might be a good time to recalibrate our perception of the world in which we live: there are times when bad guys get the glory; healthy people develop cancer; the rich lose everything; and an undeserving person wins the lottery. There are occasions when the most gifted and eligible musicians do not get recognized; talented and available athletes are overlooked; a faithful spouse loses a partner to infidelity; and a safe driver is tragically killed by a drunk driver who walks away from the accident unscathed.

Each one of us can recall events that have exposed us to the bold reality that we are powerless to control when and what circumstances will enter into our lives. Is this why we love our cinema heroes so much? Their scripted story can provide a temporary escape from our present crisis, where in the span of two hours we can fantasize that we are right there alongside our hero, overcoming impossible odds to win the day.

Is God Real and Does It Even Matter?

As the tale marches forward we cheer them on, in hopes of finding our own glint of inspiration that will embolden us to overcome what's coming against us in real life (preferably in the span of two hours). As the movie ends, reality sets back in. We do not know what tomorrow — or even the next moment — will bring with it.

This said, it is easily understandable why many people in our society who initially assume they have the power to control their own life, and then witness it begin to spin out of control, become disenchanted with the culture's characterization that *life is what we make it*. And sadly, the disenchantment often turns into bitterness and resentment.

Here's a suggestion that would be of great benefit to you. As you find yourself asking life's '*Why?*' questions, give some serious consideration to the bigger question: Could there be a God who actually cares about me, or is my existence simply a result of evolution's explanation of time plus chance (which might be better understood in everyday language as the culmination of good and bad luck)? Now, you might think that to ask a question such as this only serves as a distraction from your pressing circumstances. You consider your focus to be on a much narrower scope. You've got personal decisions to make today and a life to get on with. You don't perceive any real need to spend your time contemplating the bigger concepts regarding the purpose of your existence. But hear this, it is in your discovering the truth behind this bigger question that will provide you a more thorough understanding regarding what's going on in your life at this moment.

The topic is about life as we know it—your life—and who, if anyone, is overseeing it with any positive purpose? At this juncture, it would be erroneous to try and acquaint you with an impersonal deity whose only interest would be to oversee the major events in the world. Instead, authentic, demonstrable truth is being affirmed: There is only one God, as declared in the Bible; and this God, while exercising sovereign care over the earth, is also choreographing the details of your life, whether you are aware of it or not. Fully engaged at every level, God's intention is to maneuver you through life's circumstances into a posture where you will want to seek him out.

This God, who has openly made it known that he can be found, has also taken it upon himself to convince you to accept his invitation to enter into authentic relationship with him; something we would never want to do on our own. The mere fact that you are willing to investigate the possibility of there being only one true God is evidence enough that he is already at work in you. God's plan is to establish an indisputable awareness of his presence in both the big and small things of life. The same God who directed the prophet Moses to paint this broad stroke of truth in the Bible:

> "In the beginning God created the
> heavens and the earth."
>
> Genesis 1:1

also instructed King Solomon to record this minute certainty:

> "Man casts the lot, but its every
> decision is from the Lord."
>
> Proverbs 16:33

Here's another way of saying it—found in the New Living Translation of the Bible—which might aid in our understanding.

Is God Real and Does It Even Matter?

"We may throw the dice, but the Lord determines how they fall."
Proverbs 16:33

You might be thinking right about now, *if this were really true, everything that happens—every single circumstance, every single event that goes on in the world, as well as in my own life, down to the tiniest detail—is from the hand of God and serves a purpose, then why does everything feel so out of control?*

2.
Not Just Any God

As hostility and mistrust continue to mount throughout the world, fear has seized the opportunity to use this global insecurity as a means by which it can inject itself into our personal lives. With self-appointed media-prophets building unscalable mountains of such negative information before us, prophesying an ominous future, we find ourselves desperate to take control of something, anything, that might serve as a distraction. It is easy to see why so many are choosing to drown out the pessimism through a greater frequency in vacations and weekend getaways, passionate devotion to entertainment, sports and hobbies, and a premeditated move toward self-preservation through isolation.

It is also significant to point out that when a society permits the fear-riddled mindset of their culture to serve as the primary influencer in their reasoning process, there will always be mistaken beliefs regarding the one true God and his involvement in our lives, which is what we are witnessing today. As the population seeks relief from the increasing pressures they face, many are opting to summon their own god with the hopes that he/she/it will aid with their coping. And if one particular rendering of god doesn't do the trick, then it's on to another god, and another, and another, until a satisfactory version can be located, customized, and seamlessly blended into one's busy life.

Let's have a look at three of the more common god-constructs individuals are electing to erect in our current culture:

THE YOU-CAN-HAVE-IT-ALL GOD
Many, both in and out of the church, are choosing to promote a god who is broadly open-minded and unconditionally supportive, one who will always turn a sympathetic eye toward personal slipups and/or neglect. This person is wagering his or her eternity that this god is universalistic in nature, and will unconditionally receive everyone based on their premise that humanity's intentions are

basically good. With a carte blanche god such as this, everyone is sure to get what he or she desires, if not now, then certainly in the life to come. No one is to be rejected; no one is to be punished; no one is to be banned. For this person, God is believed to be an altruistic deity whose objectives are to: 1) give us what we want 2) refrain from demanding too much of us 3) bless all of our pursuits 4) welcome us all into heaven when we die.

THE JUST-OUT-OF-REACH GOD
Determined to keep joy and happiness just beyond our grasp, this god is perceived to be maliciously manipulating life, constantly taunting us with the unobtainable carrot before the horse. Vindictive and stingy and with a bent on getting his pound of innocent flesh out of us, this god has only one goal, to make our lives miserable. The unceasing stream of unfair circumstances in our life is all the evidence this person needs to conclude that God does not care. Helplessly subject to divine contempt, everyone is to be rejected; everyone is to be punished; and everyone is to be banned. For this person, God is an inhospitable deity who delights in withholding anything good and pleasurable from us.

THE I-PREFER-MYSELF GOD

Still, there are others who protest any version of God's existence. Convinced they can do a much better job, they have assumed the role of God, refusing to trust anyone else with the administration of their lives. Granting themselves the right to make the final determination in what is good and bad, what is moral and immoral, and what is acceptable and unacceptable, they see any external pressure to comply to another's value system as an encroachment upon their own personal rights.

Predictably, the person who would undertake the role of becoming their own god has to be constantly changing life's rules in order to keep the advantage in their favor. This is a recipe for the perfect cultural storm; namely the clashing of ethics, morals, and values in a relativistic society. The preservation and promotion of self-interest will always take precedence for the person who would be their own god. Therefore, apathy toward those outside of their circle of self-interest should be of no surprise. And from there it is just a small step to the devaluing of another's rights.

A FACT THAT CANNOT BE IGNORED

It is no secret that our pluralistic culture endorses multiple versions of God. Now, it is imperative at this juncture to understand that not everyone can be right at the same time. While *opposing* views of God are to be expected, as the Bible declares, *contradictory* views of God must be rejected. When God himself announces that he is the only God, while others in the world confidently assert there are many gods, or there is no god, or he or she is his or her own god, it needs to be understood that all of these declarations cannot be true simultaneously. Only one of those declarations can be regarded as a true statement, while all declarations in contradiction to this true statement must be regarded as false.

Ponder this for a moment: *Could it be that what lies behind every alternate version of the one true God is simply an impulse to craft a god or a non-god who would permit a person to pursue self-interest above all else?*

Whatever the motivation, this statement remains before us: *There is only one true God, or there are many gods, or there is no god.* You are being invited to test which declaration is valid. Along the way, you will also be challenged to become consistent with what you say you believe by aligning your life authentically to your findings.

As you consider this proposal, it seems best at this time—since he is the primary focus of this book—to introduce you to the One who has declared of himself to be the 'one true God'... namely, the God of the Bible.

> "For I am God, and there is no other; I am God, and there is none like Me, declaring the end from the beginning and from ancient times things not yet done saying, 'My counsel shall stand, and I will accomplish all My purpose.'"
> Isaiah 46:9-10

3.
Only One God

When a person chooses to believe in the only one true God, they are in fact rejecting all other possibilities of another god's existence. Predictably, when a conviction such as this is expressed it will open the door for all sorts of passionate objections from those who would hold a contrary opinion. It is important to recognize this fact; no matter how demanding and overbearing another person's opinion might be, an opinion on its own will never possess the power to alter what is truly right and what is truly wrong. Admittedly, while an individual's opinion might intimidate others and therefore influence the perception of truth, still, opinions alone will forever remain powerless to redefine what is true.

Therefore, because of the eternal ramifications in this particular discussion, it seems it would be in one's own best interest to consider refraining from banking his or her eternity on personal opinion alone, especially if he or she could know with certainty the truth regarding the existence of the one true God.

To put it another way, a requisite for embarking on this journey, one must be willing to table their own personal opinion in order to explore the plausibility that there is only one God, giving serious attention to what has actually been said of—and written about—the God of the Bible. This includes the recorded historical accounts of God's activity, God's demonstration of the existence of a supernatural unseen world, the fulfillment of prophesy (i.e., accuracy in foretelling future events), and the testimony of countless numbers whose lives have been supernaturally transformed. And here's the exciting part of the journey... all this evidence has been furnished for the express purpose of delivering a remarkable message: *God desires to have an authentic relationship with his creation and grant eternal life to those who would choose to believe in him!*

Now you might very well ask, "If this is the message God is trying to get out to us, why is it that so few people seem to know about it... globally speaking?" One primary reason many never hear the message is because so few who claim they possess knowledge of it are actually willing to talk about it. It's a conundrum, for sure, how a person can receive the free gift of eternal life and then opt to avoid talking about it openly. Interestingly, those same people are able to discuss at length — even with a complete stranger — their love for sports, movies, books, coffee, shopping, and music, yet when it comes to initiating a discussion about God and one's eternal destination, there seems to be an unwritten 'hands off' rule, presuming it is in everyone's best interest, for the sake of peace and harmony, to leave that subject untouched.

Fortunately, for you, that's about to change. God is going to be openly discussed here with the hopes that you'll understand what's at stake and perhaps seek out an authentic relationship with him.

First, it would be helpful to clear up some common cultural misunderstandings regarding the one true God:

• The concept of the one true God is not the result of a society's felt need to worship someone or something, instead, it is the other

way around; we who have been created by the one true God have the innate desire to worship because he placed the passion to do so within each one of us.
- The Bible is NOT a book of myths and legends—chalk-full of scribal errors—handed down through oral tradition from an ancient culture. Again and again, the Bible has been proven to be accurate, trustworthy and surprisingly practical for any man or woman willing to give it genuine consideration.
- Not all churches, synagogues, temples, shrines, or mosques believe in the same God.
- Neither individuals, nor cultures, including those who wield tremendous influence in a society are entitled to their own personal interpretation of God apart from the Bible.
- While matters of God and eternal life are personal, they were never intended to be privately kept to oneself.
- God does not take everyone to heaven nor does he send everyone to hell.

I am going to assume, because you are still reading, the following: you are roused to discover the truth regarding the validity of God's existence; you are interested in learning to what extent has God been involved in your own life up to this point; and you are curious as to what it is exactly that he wants from you from this day forward. That being said, carefully consider this question:

What would be important for you to know about God that would help your decision-making process?

And then ponder this question:

From God's perspective, what would God consider essential that you first know about him?

Thankfully, the Bible chronicles a number of historical examples of followers of God who unashamedly spoke about their faith with audiences who were largely unfamiliar with the existence of the one true God. From their recorded encounters, we can learn what is essential that a person must first accept in order to have a relationship with God.

Let's examine two particular historical narratives of a man named Paul, a devout follower of God who wrote much of the New Testament Bible. But before we get to the narratives, it would be helpful to get a little backstory on the man, Paul himself, known in his earlier days as Saul. Saul—born a Jew in

Tarsus—grew up a deeply religious man. He was schooled under the some of the greatest scholars of his day and became an outspoken advocate of Judaism. When a new group promoting a different approach to God challenged his religion, he went on the offensive and began attacking those people in hopes of destroying the movement. If he could not have them killed, at the very least he sought to have them placed in prison until they renounced their newly found faith.

During one of his journeys to the city of Damascus—with papers in hand to arrest anyone identified as a follower in this new movement—Saul experienced a life-altering event. He describes his supernatural experience as first seeing a bright light and immediately being thrown down to the ground. He goes on to testify that he heard a voice asking, "Saul, Saul, why do you persecute me?" When he inquired to whom it was speaking to him, there was the reply, "I am Jesus whom you are persecuting." Stricken suddenly with blindness (scales appeared, covering his eyes), Saul found himself helpless. Now at the mercy of his fellow travelers, they helped him get to Damascus. The Spirit of God then instructed Paul, once he arrived in the city, to wait until he was told what he should do. Refusing food and water, Paul kept to himself until a man named Ananias, who was sent from God, showed up on his doorstep. Ananias shared a message that would change the entire course of Saul's life. The message Saul—now to be called Paul—heard and responded to is the very same message being discussed in this book.

Paul, now transformed from within, became a passionate advocate, able defender, and a voluminous writer for this life-changing message. He willingly suffered rejection from his former teachers and was viciously persecuted by his religious peers. In spite of this, he stayed the course, sharing the message with anyone willing to listen. He desired that everyone personally experience what he had experienced. The remainder of his life was spent traveling to different cities throughout Asia Minor, seizing opportunities to dialogue with men and women who were pursuing religion like he had been. But his primary mission was to converse with those who were fully preoccupied with the demands of their culture and unaware of the one true God.

Is God Real and Does It Even Matter?

We now come to the two historical narratives involving the apostle Paul. Please read over both passages carefully [*my italics below*].

"Now at Lystra there was a man sitting who could not use his feet. He was crippled from birth and had never walked. He listened to Paul speaking. And Paul, looking intently at him and seeing that he had faith to be made well, said in a loud voice, "Stand upright on your feet." And he sprang up and began walking. And when the crowds saw what Paul had done, they lifted up their voices, saying in Lycaonian, "The gods have come down to us in the likeness of men!" Barnabas they called Zeus, and Paul, Hermes, because he was the chief speaker. And the priest of Zeus, whose temple was at the entrance to the city, brought oxen and garlands to the gates and wanted to offer sacrifice with the crowds. But when the apostles Barnabas and Paul heard of it, they tore their garments and rushed out into the crowd, crying out, "*Men, why are you doing these things? We also are men, of like nature with you, and we bring you good news,*

> *that you should turn from these vain things to a living God, who made the heaven and the earth and the sea and all that is in them. In past generations he allowed all the nations to walk in their own ways. Yet he did not leave himself without witness, for he did good by giving you rains from heaven and fruitful seasons, satisfying your hearts with food and gladness."*"
>
> Acts 14:11-17

Here's the second narrative account of the apostle Paul sharing his faith in God while visiting Athens, Greece [*my italics below*].

> "So Paul, standing in the midst of the Areopagus, said: "*Men of Athens, I perceive that in every way you are very religious. For as I passed along and observed the objects of your worship, I found also an altar with this inscription, 'To the unknown god.' What therefore you worship as unknown, this I proclaim to you. The God who made the world and everything in it, being Lord of heaven and earth, does not live in temples made by man, nor is he served by human hands, as though he needed anything, since he*

himself gives to all mankind life and breath and everything. And he made from one man every nation of mankind to live on all the face of the earth, having determined allotted periods and the boundaries of their dwelling place, that they should seek God, and perhaps feel their way toward him and find him. Yet he is actually not far from each one of us, for

'In him we live and move and have our being';

as even some of your own poets have said,

'For we are indeed his offspring.'

Being then God's offspring, we ought not to think that the divine being is like gold or silver or stone, an image formed by the art and imagination of man. The times of ignorance God overlooked, but now he commands all people everywhere to repent, because he has fixed a day on which he will judge the world in righteousness by a man whom he has appointed; and of this he has given assurance to all by raising him from the dead."

Acts 17:22-31

Is God Real and Does It Even Matter?

If you were aroused at any level as you read over these accounts, rest assured; God is at work to get your attention. This is a good thing. But note if you felt or sensed nothing, you are still being encouraged to continue reading. God is not in the business of enlightening seekers the exact same way through the exact same circumstances every time. God did not create men and women to be fatalistic robots, predictable and mechanical. God has made you to be uniquely you, personality and all. Listen to how David, King of Israel, describes God's creative handiwork at play in the singular design of every man, woman and child on earth:

> "For you [God] formed my inward parts; you knitted me together in my mother's womb. I praise you, for I am fearfully and wonderfully made. Wonderful are your works; my soul knows it very well."
> Psalm 139:13-14

What we see in King David's summation, '*my soul knows it very well*,' is an expression of deep, heartfelt gratitude for being privy to an intimate understanding of his own existence and the life-changing experience of a personal relationship with his God.

There isn't a person alive that wouldn't want to possess this type of inner confidence, to be able to know with certainty the real reason for their existence... and to be able to *know it very well*; that he or she has been uniquely created, fearfully and wonderfully made, and that his or her life has significant purpose and meaning beyond the mundane demands and unexpected afflictions of everyday life.

Interestingly, while each of us remain unique and our life journeys varied, we are told that we all have the same starting point; that for every man or woman who would desire to experience this intimate awareness of God, self and purpose, he or she must, without exception, begin with a simple, yet profound, expression of belief as laid out in this truth statement from the book of Hebrews:

> "Whoever would draw near to God must believe that he exists and that he rewards those who seek him."
>
> Hebrews 11:6

Is God Real and Does It Even Matter?

Would you include yourself amongst those who say they believe in God? It is no secret that the polls indicate that the majority of people today still possess a belief in some sort of god or higher power. But the word, believe, used here in Hebrews as well as throughout the entire Bible carries with it a much more expansive meaning than mere mental ascent to God's existence. James, another follower of Jesus who penned what is known as the book of James, put it this way:

> "You believe that God is one; you do well. Even the demons believe—and shudder!"
>
> James 2:19

James is making the point that it is never enough for a person to just *say* they believe in God. The nominal acquiescence described in the verse above will change nothing in a person's life, barring a few sentimental expressions when they are in certain circles. Contrasted with the mere statement of a belief in God's existence, the Bible wants to introduce us to a belief that is genuinely effectual… a faith that can initiate authentic transformation right now, as well as redirect one's eternal future.

4.
What It Means to Believe in God

From a simple review of the apostle Paul's dialogue with the culture of his day, a person can begin to understand what it takes to have a genuine relationship with God. It starts with a key premise that every person must be willing to accept as true in order for belief to be authentic and transformational.

To believe in God means one must acknowledge him as their Creator.

In the first account of Paul's narrative he declares: "*...you should turn from these vain things to a living God, who made the heaven and the earth and the sea and all that is in them.*" In the second account, he puts it this way: "*The God who made the world and everything in it, being Lord of heaven and earth, does not live in temples made by man, nor is he served by human hands, as though he needed anything, since he *himself gives to all mankind life and breath and everything."*

This most basic truth, God is the Creator of all things, is non-negotiable and is where every single person must begin if they want to know the one true God. Paul's point of entry with anyone unfamiliar with the one true God was to first introduce the person to the reality that God is alive and active; therefore, he is the Author of all life. Paul announces God to be both the Creator who has made everyone and everything, as well as the Lord of all, which means this God is the one who is in control of all things. For Paul, it was of primary importance to properly introduce his listeners to the truth about their Creator, and only then offer him or her the opportunity to turn and follow this God rather than go their own way.

Paul, like the myriads of followers preceding him, accepted Genesis 1:1, the first verse in the Bible, as authentic truth: *"In the beginning God created the heavens and the earth."* Let's take it a step further... believing in God as our supernatural Creator is the requisite for believing and accepting the rest of the message God has for us. Why is that? Think about it, if the first simple statement in the

Bible about God cannot be trusted, it would be unreasonable to trust the remainder of the message. It's that important and why every single person must start with that simple, yet profound Truth.

Let's go yet a little further. Did you know that everyone has an inner awareness of God's existence, regardless of his or her upbringing? Whether they will readily admit it or not, is another thing altogether. The apostle Paul penned this truth in Romans chapter one. In context, he is addressing all of humanity, which means there is no one who is excluded from this reality:

> "For what can be known about God is plain to them [humanity], because God has shown it to them. For his invisible attributes, namely, his eternal power and divine nature, have been clearly perceived, ever since the creation of the world, in the things that have been made. So they [humanity] are without excuse."
>
> Romans 1:19-20

If this is true, then why do individuals go to such great lengths to build a case for denying

God's existence? Why is the world littered with excuses, if we really have no excuse? That is the heart of the matter.

Let's revisit Paul's statement at Lystra in Acts 14: "*In past generations he allowed all the nations to walk in their own ways. Yet he did not leave himself without witness, for he did good by giving you rains from heaven and fruitful seasons, satisfying your hearts with food and gladness.*" And in Acts 17, Paul states: "*The times of ignorance God overlooked, but now he commands all people everywhere to repent, because he has fixed a day on which he will judge the world in righteousness...*"

Note that once Paul introduces God as the one true Lord and Creator he then begins to set the stage for why things exist as they do and what must happen in order for lasting transformation to come about in a person's life. He does this by faithfully opening a window to the Truth, reminding us of our past opposition, which explains our present condition, and thus exposes our need for a sovereign remedy in order to recast our eternal position.

An important truth should not be overlooked here; it is explicitly stated in the text that God is remarkably compassionate, full of goodness and extremely patient with us. He is portrayed as providing for our needs when we didn't deserve it, satisfying us with food and gladness, and overlooking times of ignorance when we chose self-interest above all else. Paul announces to his listeners that what God has in fact been doing is restraining his judgment while simultaneously caring for us... all this with an express purpose in mind, so we can have the opportunity to enter into an eternal relationship with him.

Taking into account the surety of a coming judgment, it is essential to note that this message comes with a timetable. While the gracious offer from God is on the table today, there is no guarantee that it will be there tomorrow, which is why Paul implores everyone who hears to accept the offer while it still exists, before it is too late.

Again, if this is the case, having now been made aware of whom God is and how compassionate he has been with us up to this point, and if a final judgment is really coming, why don't we all run to accept his wonderful invitation to be forgiven and restored, and thus escape judgment?

5.
Why the World Doesn't Believe

Paul identifies the world's resolve to avert its attention away from God in Romans chapter one and verse eighteen (the passage we read earlier that stated we are left without excuse):

> "For the wrath of God is revealed from heaven against all ungodliness and unrighteousness of men, who by their unrighteousness suppress the truth."
> Romans 1:18

Notice it says by *their unrighteous condition* the world attempts to bury the truth of God's existence from everyone's sight. So, to whom is the Bible referring to when it speaks of those who are unrighteous? Bank robbers? Serial killers? Rapists? Pedophiles? Abusers? Did you know that to be considered a participant in unrighteousness all one need do is falter on one or more of God's moral requirements? The slightest infraction in areas such as: lying, cheating, stealing, hating, lust, envy, greed, gossip, slander, selfishness, ignoring the needs of others, and simple disobedience, is sufficient grounds to place a person into the category of being unrighteous? The biblical author James puts it this way:

> "For whoever keeps the whole law but fails in one point has become accountable for all of it."
> James 2:10

To be candid, this truth leaves no one out of the picture. We are all considered partners in unrighteousness. But the world rebuffs the thought of being profiled together and categorized as unrighteous; thus, refusing to be held to such standards, it searches tirelessly for new ways to devalue the presence of a Creator who would hold his creation accountable.

Do you remember what you did as a child when you wanted the bogeyman to disappear? You merely covered your eyes and plugged your ears, assuming that if you couldn't see or hear it, that it wasn't really there or would vanish from your presence.

This simple illustration from the life of a child is an excellent picture of what we attempt to do as adults with the truth that God has revealed to us.

While the formula to force God out of the picture as adults might differ from a child's effort to be rid of the bogeyman, still the passion to reject the reality of God's existence is evident under the guise of what is believed to be far more noble and worthwhile pursuits such as: wealth and investment, science and technology, health and medicine, education and advancement, the arts and entertainment, political and public service, etc., and if these aren't effective enough to drown out God's reality, we will reach for anything that will numb our conscience.

Interestingly, when Paul measures the sum of society's self-preoccupation against the opportunity to pursue and know the God of the universe, he calls their efforts, at best, vain pursuits. You recall in the first account he states, "*...we bring you good news, that you should turn from these vain things to a living God...*" And in the second account he puts it this way, "*Being then God's offspring, we ought not to think that the divine being is like gold or* *silver or stone, an image formed by the art and imagination of man."*

God is being introduced as the Creator who is wholly different from any representation a person could conjure up in this world. Paul reasons that we possess nothing in our seemingly endless resources with which we can compare the living God. He is that different.

Paul then informs his hearers that the human race in fact exists as a result of being God's own offspring. In other words, the Bible states every man woman and child is here because of God, having been created in his image. And it is because we have his fingerprint on our lives that our Creator has taken the initiative to establish a way, in spite of our continued resistance, for us to find our way to him and thus experience real life both now and forevermore.

Still, most openly reject this truth and all-too-quickly regard any man or woman who would choose to believe in this sort of God as someone to be pitied. People who accept the living God as their Creator are deemed by the masses to be backwoods, uneducated, and uninformed with what's really happening in the world. Thus, we are witnessing a concerted effort by our culture to squelch the voice of Christians with white noise and marginalize the lives of those who say they follow the God of the Bible.

The world's reaction is predictable, and thus brings us to our own personal rub with the idea of God's existence.

6.
Why We Don't Believe

The thought of personal accountability to someone other than one's own self for how we choose to live is the fundamental reason people object to God's existence and his sovereign control over us. The basic assumption is that any and all monitoring of one's personal lifestyle belongs solely to the person making the choices. Our boss might exercise limited control over us in the workplace, or our professor/teacher in the classroom, or even our parents in the home, but we are free to quit, drop out, or move out if we don't like the environment, and thus terminate the relationship(s). To confess that one believes in the living God of the Bible elevates the notion of personal accountability to another whole level, not only because it means we agree there is consequential fruit for our daily thoughts, words and actions, but it also creates an acute awareness that what we choose to produce in this life will be the harvest of our eternity.

While our culture continues to promote a spirit of entitlement—determined to convince us that we are inherently a commendable people and have every right to control all aspects of our life without any fear of eternal consequences—God tells us a different story. Let's look at a few verses in the Bible that help clarify who really is in control:

> "Now we know that whatever the law says it speaks to those who are under the law, so that every mouth may be stopped, and the whole world may be held accountable to God."
> Romans 3:19

> "I tell you, on the day of judgment people will give account for every careless word they speak, for by your words you will be justified, and by your words you will be condemned."
> Matthew 12:36-37

> "I the LORD search the heart and test the mind, to give every man according

to his ways, according to the fruit of his deeds."

Jeremiah 17:10

"Nothing is covered up that will not be revealed, or hidden that will not be known. Therefore whatever you have said in the dark shall be heard in the light, and what you have whispered in private rooms shall be proclaimed on the housetops."

Luke 12:2-3

It is important to understand that God has revealed to us that he is the only one who has, is, and will continue to decide what happens in life. He is the one who sets the standard of conduct for all humankind that will ultimately determine each person's destiny. God, the Bible says, will hold every single one of us accountable. No one is excused. No one gets a free pass.

We struggle with this truth because the world's spirit of entitlement seems so much more appealing, assuring us that we are intrinsically deserving, that we have personal rights, and need not feel guilty for pursuing self-gratification. This world's spirit of entitlement pledges that we answer to no one.

Hearing for the first time that we are not inherently as good as we prefer to think we are can be a very difficult concept to accept, and indeed many will refuse to believe it. To admit that our take on life over the span of a lifetime has been inherently skewed, plagued with misinformation regarding our spiritual condition, can be arduous. Yet, this is what God has declared to us all. To further illustrate this truth, consider this reversal: while America's Bill of Rights state that every citizen is to be presumed innocent until proven guilty, the Bible has declared just the opposite for the human race; every man and woman—which includes you and me—has been declared guilty and now find themselves in need of a miracle; we desperately need God to declare us no longer guilty. Asserting, "But I've got my rights!" will not get the job done. Claiming we are really a good soul down deep inside will have no effect on the one who is the impartial judge of the world and all that is in it. Understanding this basic concept of our global guilt helps provide clarity and understanding of why things are happening as they are.

Is God Real and Does It Even Matter?

You might object, *but I haven't really done anything so terrible that I would classify it as evil.* Admittedly, when we think of evil, we tend to compare our relatively mild misbehavior against the vilest of crimes others have committed and therefore find no problem in pronouncing ourselves, although not perfect, as being pretty good, or at the very least, not really that bad. But here is reality: did you know that every motive with selfish intention, every spoken lie whether big or small, black or white, every impulse to be dishonest, every undertone of gossip, every secret thought of envy, every act of unkindness or whisper of judgment, is all the evidence needed to reveal that you and I are already guilty and therefore have a personal appearance date on God's docket where we will stand accountable before him? This can be quite unsettling. It makes a person squirm. Our flesh repels the thought that personal choices made in the moment can have such impacting consequences on our eternity. Yet, this is the universal experience before God. Listen to what Paul says in Romans chapter three [*my italics below*]:

"None is righteous, *no, not one*;
no one understands;

no one seeks for God.
All have turned aside; together they have become worthless;
no one does good,
not even one."

Romans 3:10-12

"For there is no distinction: for *all have sinned* and fall short of the glory of God."

Romans 3:22-23

Paul is stating a hard but inescapable truth; because of our initial condition, even our best efforts put forth will never be good enough. We are all guilty sinners without degrees of exception. There is no such thing as a good sinner and a bad sinner in God's economy. In fact, a writer of the Old Testament named Isaiah describes the truism this way:

"We have all become like one who is unclean,
    and all our righteous deeds are like a polluted garment.
We all fade like a leaf,
    and our iniquities, like the wind, take us away."

Isaiah 64:6

Is God Real and Does It Even Matter?

It is obvious to anyone who chooses to read the Bible that its message does not muddy the waters when it comes to describing the human condition apart from God. It doesn't cower from asserting personal guilt for a person's choosing to go his or her own way. Its record is crystal clear; with guilt comes the consequence of a sentence of condemnation.

Now, will ignoring this difficult truth make God go away? Will pleading ignorance provide a person the proverbial 'get out of jail' card? Will actively denying our guilt alter reality? The answer is no, no, and no.

Then, you may ask, what are my options as one who stands with everyone else as guilty before God?

7.
Understanding What is at Stake

Before considering your options, it is important to first address the meaning of three key words used throughout this book: **unrighteous**, **guilt** and **sin**. Their biblical definitions can overlap at certain junctures, but still, each word carries with it its own meaning. I want to make sure you clearly understand the intended significance of each of these words as our culture—a culture who refuses to accept the Bible as the authority on truth—blindly stabs at redefining or even removing these words from our vocabulary.

To start, when the Bible says that we are all **unrighteous**, it speaks of our dismantled relationship with God. Men and women apart from God do not have a right standing with him, therefore we are all considered out of relationship with him. We are unrighteous. You may—and rightly should—be asking, 'Is there a way to be made righteous before him so I can experience a proper relationship with him before it is too late?' The answer is a resounding, YES!

Next, when the Bible mentions our **guilt** it is referring to our justly deserving condemnation. In God's legal system he is truly both Judge and Jury and has rendered a verdict of, 'Guilty,' for all mankind. To be declared guilty means the evidence has been sufficient to convict and it is imminent that the guilty parties (you and I) will be receiving what they deserve. You may—and rightly should—be asking, 'Is there a way I can have my guilty verdict reversed before my sentence is carried out?' The answer is a resounding, YES!

Lastly, when the Bible refers to **sin**, it actually has one of two thoughts in mind, depending upon its context. But before we discuss these two thoughts, a basic question needs to be asked: Where did sin originate? You recall Paul's statement in Acts 17: *"And he made from one man every nation of mankind to live on all the face of the earth."* That 'one man' Paul is referring to is the historical figure, Adam. He is the first human being. In the book of Genesis, we read of Adam and Eve being created and the relationship they experienced with God. We are told in the narrative that in order to keep the relationship intact forever, there was a stipulation placed upon Adam and Eve; they had to obey a simple command God gave them. As the biblical account goes, Adam, wanting to go his own way, chose instead to take his chances and disobey. And this is how sin entered the world. We also discover in the Bible that Adam's choice to disobey had a direct effect on his progeny (you and me). The consequence of his disobedience was death, first for Adam, and then for all who would come from Adam. To put it plainly, death is the penalty for sin. Listen to Paul's description of sin's universal effect in Romans chapter five:

> "Therefore, just as sin came into the world through one man, and death through sin, and so death spread to all men because all sinned."
>
> Romans 5:12

No one can escape the fact that he or she is a sinner. We are all sinners, equally guilty before God. What is the indisputable evidence that sin resides in us all? We all die. There is really no such thing as death by natural causes. There is nothing natural in death. Death is the non-negotiable wage set by God to be distributed equally to a disobedient humanity for sin.

Now to the important discussion of the two concepts of sin as mentioned in the Bible: First, sin is referred to as an inward condition of the individual. All humankind, because of Adam's sin, carries with them a sin nature from birth. It is in our spiritual DNA. Once again, the evidence it is there is death. It is important to note once again that even our best intended overtures of doing good are actually considered not good because of this sin nature that resides in each of us. Without God, it is inevitable that this sin nature in us will reveal who we really are, rebellious men and women who really want nothing to do with their Creator.

Second, sin is also described in other places as an outward act of disobedience or lawlessness arising from an inward bent of self-interest. We can't get around this; because we come from Adam we are destined to make sinful choices because we have a sinful, self-serving heart. One improper word, thought or action is all the evidence needed to prove that a sinful nature resides in us. Without God, sin is what we do. It is who we are. Whether it is an unspoken lust for something we see, or a secret inward desire for personal gratification, or a self-centered effort to become someone to be admired by others, all of it is sin. And it is because of sin that we find ourselves wholly without excuse before God. You may—and rightly should—be asking, 'Is there a way to have my sins removed and thus be clean and free of sin?' The answer is a resounding, YES!

8.
The Solution to Our Dilemma

If you were made aware that I had in my possession the only cure for terminal cancer and that I was choosing to keep it to myself, what sort of person would you consider me to be? For anyone to selfishly withhold such a life-altering remedy from the millions whose restorative health depended upon it would be, without a doubt, sheer travesty. The cure for such a deadly disease, if ever found, should never be kept secret, instead it should be shouted from the rooftops. Even those who were not immediately aware that deadly cancer cells had invaded their bodies would stand to benefit. For them to ignore the signs of cancer or even deny its existence in their own life would not be the solution, especially if a cure were readily available.

In the same fashion, if I possessed the remedy for the complete removal of sin in a person and I knew how to lead them onto the path to eternal life, and decided to keep this life-changing information to myself, would that not also be a travesty? It is critical to understand that sin, while universal in nature, is also terminal. Ignoring the signs of sin in our lives or succumbing to denying its existence is not the solution when the remedy is readily available.

What is God's remedy?

Let's revisit Paul's discourse in Athens in Acts 17: "*but now he [God] commands all people everywhere to repent...*"

Note a number of important truths stated in Paul's text:
1. The words, *but now*, are used to indicate that the time for action has arrived. This is not something to be delayed or put off.
2. Next, the words, *he [God] commands*, reminds us that this action we are told to take is not optional, but is an imperative to be obeyed without hesitation.
3. Next, the words, *all people everywhere*, tells us who the intended audience is, everyone in the world without exception.
4. Lastly, the phrase, *to repent*, reveals God's prescribed remedy Paul is now introducing.

Is God Real and Does It Even Matter?

The message Paul is sharing is not complicated; in order to receive a not guilty verdict—and to experience forgiveness, restoration and authentic relationship with the one true God—we must repent. Let me explain it another way; to be declared not guilty by God, one must be willing to first admit personal guilt, to receive forgiveness of sin, one must confess they are a sinner in need of forgiveness, and to fully experience a right relationship with God one must admit that he or she has had a broken relationship with God.

So, if repentance is the key to having our unrighteousness made righteous, our guilt being satisfied and our sin removed, it might be helpful to know what the word actually means, and what genuine repentance looks like. As God's only remedy, it is imperative that repentance be discussed in some detail, not only because of its importance, but also because the word has come to mean so many different things to people today. Some hear the word, repent, and immediately think negative thoughts; they envision a person screaming at passersby on a street corner. Others, acutely aware of their personal failings, become overwhelmed when they hear the word, repent. They can't get beyond repeating, 'I repent,' and as a result of being stalled on this statement, they've never been able to experience the next step... the reality of being truly forgiven. Still others have never really considered the word, repent, until now and therefore need assistance in properly understanding what it means. No doubt, discerning what *to repent* means is essential, for it is the next step on the path to an authentic relationship with God, the first being to personally believe in God's existence as our Creator.

Question: So how do you know if you've truly repented? In order to discover what authentic repentance is and to remove any confusion on the matter, let's first look at what repentance is not.

• Repentance is not your personal key to getting out of trouble.
• Repentance is not your go-to for ridding yourself of bad feelings.
• Repentance is not resolving to turn over a new leaf in life.
• Repentance is not your provisional 'protection from hell insurance policy.'

9.
The Recipe for Relationship

While repentance has a single intended meaning, it is important to understand that it may be experienced in any number of ways in an individual. There is no particular verbal formula one must articulate that will trigger repentance and thus initiate a right relationship with God. Some people are able to verbally express in great detail their present condition and their desperate need for God. Still, others on the other end of the spectrum find it hard to formulate enough words to make a single sentence. They have an inexpressible sorrow deep in their soul that has been prompted by this new awareness of their sin. They are acutely mindful of their need for God to do something transformative in their life. They just don't know how to say it.

Which of these two people pleases God? Both do. We must understand that repentance is not the proper accumulation of words, or the lack thereof that matter to God. Repentance is always an issue of the heart.

This said, it is still essential for us to gain a proper understanding what it means for a person to truly repent, for if you don't understand what repentance is, how will you know when you've repented? How will you know it is authentic?

It might be helpful to understand repentance in the same manner as one might make a cake from scratch. A cake from scratch involves certain essential ingredients and a sequential order in which those ingredients are to be added. Leave any of the ingredients out of the mix, such as baking powder or sugar or eggs, and the cake will never become a cake no matter how long you leave it in the oven. A baker also follows a sequence, mixing all the dry ingredients together and then slowly adding the wet ingredients. Bottom-line, one must have certain essential ingredients and a sequence to follow if one expects to end up with a cake.

In similar fashion, you could say that repentance possesses four essential ingredients. Attempt to leave any of these ingredients out and you'll end up with something less than true repentance. The four ingredients are:

1. **Conviction**
2. **Confession**
3. **Reconciliation**
4. **Redirection**

Note these four ingredients are also sequential. They must be experienced in this order for a right relationship with God to be cultivated. The Bible offers a lot of insight so we can properly embrace what each of these mean as we move toward God. Let's look at each one briefly.

10.
The First Ingredient: Conviction

When we speak of this first ingredient we need to understand there are basically two types of conviction a person may experience. The first type of conviction is the person who feels badly for something they have done that they knew was wrong. They are embarrassed and fearful that their disobedience may be exposed, which would result in getting into trouble. With their hand freshly out of the cookie jar, they are hasty to make all sorts of promises that it will never ever happen again. This type of conviction is purely circumstantial and wholly dependent upon whether or not they think what they have done is wrong. If they are not found out, there can be little or no remorse. This is not the type of conviction God considers authentic.

Let me see if I can illustrate this first type of conviction by way of personal example. For the first five years of my life I lived in a little guest house on my grandparents' acreage with my mom and younger sibling. I'll never forget my next-door neighbor, Larry Keith Manning, who was my best friend.

One day Larry Keith Manning (that's what I called him) and I were playing in the gravel driveway in front of our home. As two rambunctious little boys, our play quickly escalated to a point of conducting a pretend war. Our weapons of choice were anything within reach... namely, the gravel in the driveway. In an effort to gain the upper hand I jumped up into the bed of my grandfather's Chevy pick-up truck. Larry Keith Manning, in an effort to do the same, jumped up on the trunk of my mother's new Kaiser sedan.

As we hurled rocks (pretend grenades) at each other, one of my projectiles struck squarely in the rear window of my mom's car, shattering the glass. Larry Keith Manning looked at the window, then looked at me and said, "I need to go home."

Feeling horrible for what I had done, I did what any normal kid would do, I ran and hid behind the house, hoping no one would find out. As my uncle was returning from the playing in the creek on the back of the property, he saw me huddled up in the corner of the house sobbing. He asked what was wrong. I didn't say anything so he continued walking around to the front of the house. Seconds later he reappeared giggling and jumping and pointing at me saying, "I know what you did. You're in so much trouble!"

Here's the point of my illustration. At that moment of crisis in my life I was not concerned about my standing with God. I was not aware that I had sinned against him. The only thing I was concerned about was hoping my mom would somehow, some way... not find out. I felt awful (as awful as a five-year-old could feel), but I was not preoccupied with any type of conviction initiated by God. I just felt badly that I had done something for which I was going to get into trouble.

The second type of conviction is different. It is a profound sorrow of the heart and soul. This person is not concerned with what anyone else thinks about him or her. This type of conviction is the graphic realization that he or she is out sync with his or her Creator. They understand, at some level, what it is they have done by personally rejecting their God, and they are fearfully crushed knowing that they deserve the worst. We have a couple of examples of people in the Bible who experienced this type of conviction. Note they are also on both ends of the expressive spectrum.

In the first passage King David expresses his conviction in detail for choosing his own sinful self-interest over God's clear instructions. He realizes that what he did was morally wrong and now he was experiencing the fallout, a sorrowful conviction in the depths of his being that is wreaking havoc on everyday life. He did not care what others thought about his disobedience. He was focused solely on what was God's assessment of the situation. For David, God was the only thing that mattered. Listen to his heart as he eloquently expresses it in poetic phrases:

> "For when I kept silent, my bones
> wasted away
>   through my groaning all day long.
> For day and night your hand was
> heavy upon me;
>   my strength was dried up as by the
> heat of summer."
> Psalm 32:3-4

In the second passage, we have a publican/tax collector, otherwise known as a cultural outcast, who cannot even raise his head. He is experiencing inexpressible sorrow. Listen to his heart:

> "But the tax collector, standing far off, would not even lift up his eyes to heaven, but beat his breast..."
>
> Luke 18:13

I hope you can see what both of these men were experiencing. They both had arrived at the exact same place of understanding; each was guilty before God. Neither could escape it. They could not stand up under the pressure of biblical conviction. And to ignore it and try to move on in life would only make things worse. So, rather than ignore biblical conviction, they choose to add the second ingredient.

11.
The Second Ingredient: Confession

To experience the pressure of conviction without the release valve of confession could drive a person to utter despair. As we witnessed in David's description, the longer you put off dealing with biblical conviction the more painful life becomes. It affected David's sleeping, his strength and ability to think clearly. The dryness went to the soul. It is obvious both men were desperate to get the proverbial elephant off their chest. And it was heartfelt, penitent confession that would be the ticket. When preceded by biblical conviction, confession is truly refreshing to the soul. To experience one without the other would be like trying to make a cake without flour, which would not really be a cake at all. We must also remember that confession, although expressed with words, remains an issue of the heart.

Look over King David's confession when he finally decided to surrender to God, acting upon the conviction he was experiencing:

> "I acknowledged my sin to you,
>   and I did not cover my iniquity;
> I said, "I will confess my transgressions
> to the LORD,"
>   and you forgave the iniquity of my
> sin."
>
> Psalm 32:5

In the same manner, but expressed more simply, the publican/tax collector also acted upon the conviction he was experiencing:

> "But the tax collector, standing far off, would not even lift up his eyes to heaven, but beat his breast, saying, 'God, be merciful to me, a sinner!' I tell you, this man went down to his house justified."
>
> Luke 18:13-14

Each person's word choices were so different. One was able to pen his expressions eloquently, while the other man was only able to verbalize a single sentence.

Is God Real and Does It Even Matter?

I recall an experience like this in my own life during my first year of ministry. Having just graduated from seminary I labored unsuccessfully to cope with the conviction that during my last semester I had cheated on an exam. I felt horrible... I felt hypocritical. How could I teach about integrity if I did not live with integrity? While not a habitual pattern in my life, but rather a wrong decision in the moment, still, it was a bad decision.

Here is the backstory. I had been given the opportunity to make up a test in Hebrew for which I had not prepared. Sitting in a small room unproctored with the test in front of me, I did the unthinkable. Fearful I would fail, I pulled out my textbook and copied answers to the questions I could not answer. I rationalized that I would only look up answers to half the test. I received a B- on the test rather than a dreaded D or F.

Fast-forward nine months and two thousand miles from school... I am now unable to pray, eat or sleep. The conviction of what I had done was bearing down hard on me. Finally, I broke down and confessed it to God, promising that I would do whatever it took to make it right. That said, I knew I had to make the call to my professor. Over the phone I explained the situation in detail. I came clean and told him I knew I deserved the worst and that I would take the test again or take an F. With tenderness in his voice, he reminded me I was not the first one to do this and that he truly appreciated the call and my personal confession. He suggested that we leave things as they were and learn from this going forward. He assured me that he held no animosity toward me, but instead, admired the courage I had to make the call and asked me to please keep in touch.

Once again, I felt clean. The weight of my guilt was off my shoulders. All was good. My conscience was clear. I was free and light as a feather.

My professor did not have to be so kind, but he was. And like both men in the verses above, I received what I did not deserve, which is the third ingredient.

12.
The Third Ingredient: Reconciliation

I've never been a big follower of the theater, but I know enough about scripts and how essential they are in helping a director prepare for a successful performance. First, it is critical that a playwright provide a cast of characters so one can know who is taking part in the play. Second, there needs to be an easy-to-follow dialogue so the readers can perform their part, knowing what to say and when to say it. Third, there needs to be clearly timed stage directions, like, "Enter *CHARACTER* stage left," and "Exit *CHARACTER* stage right."

I would like to borrow some script terminology, if I may, as it is time to introduce a new character to the story God has told mankind. His name is Jesus. One could even go so far as to provide a stage directive, "Enter Jesus stage above."

Is God Real and Does It Even Matter?

While you may have heard the name of Jesus uttered in various settings, some religious and some not so religious, it is important that you know the plain truth about him and become familiar with the purpose of his character in God's story. To do this, we need to acquaint ourselves with six established facts about Jesus. While there is much more to the historical figure, Jesus, these six basic truths will help explain why God has declared him to be the only way to experience true forgiveness, restoration and eternal life. These six facts about Jesus are:

1. He is the Infinite God-Man
2. As a son, he lived in perfect obedience
3. Although innocent of any crime or wrongdoing, he was cruelly beaten and hung upon a cross to die
4. On the third day after his death, he was raised supernaturally from the dead
5. Forty-days after his resurrection, he visibly ascended into heaven
6. God promises that he will return one day soon to judge the living and the dead

Before we touch on each of these truths, I want to clear up something about the use of the name 'Jesus' itself. The name 'Jesus' means in its most basic sense, 'God saves.' Often when people say the name 'Jesus' they attach the word, 'Christ,' to it. Thus, many have come to assume the name 'Christ' is a type of last name of 'Jesus.' That is not the case. In New Testament times people, along with their given names, were normally identified as either a 'son of' someone or associated with the town from which they held residence. Note a disciple of Jesus named Peter, was also called, 'Simon Bar-Jonah,' which means he was the son (bar is the Hebrew word for son) of a man named Jonah. In the case of 'Jesus' he is often referred to as 'Jesus of Nazareth,' because Nazareth was where he had lived at a certain juncture of his life. So, when one says the name, 'Jesus,' it is important to understand that the name 'Christ' is not his surname; no, it is actually a title. The word 'Christ' means 'Anointed,' which comes from the Hebrew word, 'Messiah.' Normally in the original language of the New Testament, a definite article is used before the title word 'Christ.' So, a better reading or translation would be 'Jesus, the Christ.' It is important to understand in the scope of God's story that the human name 'Jesus' was given to indicate the purpose of his entering this world, that being 'to Save,' and that the word 'Christ' was the royal title actually bestowed upon him by his heavenly Father.

Now let's examine briefly how each of these truths impact our being reconciled to God.

Fact #1 About Jesus - He is the Infinite God-Man

Note that the stage directive was, "Enter Jesus stage above." There is a reason it was stated in this manner. It is helpful to know that Jesus is also referred to as the Infinite God-Man. In basic terms, what this means is that Jesus, having been seated for eternity past at the right hand of the Father as the Son of God, is fully God, while at the same time, having been born of a virgin circa 3 BC, became fully Man. When Jesus entered into this world through his mother, Mary, God sovereignly protected the human nature of Jesus through the Holy Spirit, so that he was conceived without sin. Note Jesus is the only person who has ever been born without a sin nature. This is one of those mysteries biblical scholars throughout the centuries have tried to comprehend and explain. For the purpose of this book, it is enough to believe this truth because God has declared it to be so in his

Word. Why is it important that we know this? You'll see here in a moment. For now, read over these verses. They can help shore up our understanding of reconciliation.

> "Though he was in the form of God, did not count equality with God a thing to be grasped, but emptied himself, by taking the form of a servant, being born in the likeness of men."
>
> Philippians 2:6-7

> "He is the image of the invisible God, the firstborn of all creation. For by him all things were created, in heaven and on earth, visible and invisible, whether thrones or dominions or rulers or authorities—all things were created through him and for him."
>
> Colossian 1:15-16

> "Now the birth of Jesus Christ took place in this way. When his mother Mary had been betrothed [engaged] to Joseph, before they came together she was found to be with child from the Holy Spirit."
>
> Matthew 1:18

In God's story, aka the Theater of Life, timing is everything. Jesus entered the world sinless at the exact moment God had planned, even predicting it centuries before with precise accuracy down to the tiniest detail. And what Jesus did once he was here being even more miraculous.

Fact #2 About Jesus - As a son, he lived in perfect obedience

Historically, we don't know much about the childhood and teen years of Jesus. In fact, we are kept pretty much in the dark regarding his early adult life until he reaches approximately thirty years of age. The Gospel accounts of Matthew, Mark, Luke and John record many of the details of what went on in his life after the age of thirty. This much we do know from the Biblical record, Jesus was able to live his entire life in this sin-laden world without sinning. For us, that task has proven to be impossible because of our sin nature. We can never be sinless through our own determination and effort. But for Jesus, who was born without sin, this possibility became a reality through his obedience, of which mankind would benefit greatly. Why is it important to know this truth about Jesus? In order for men and women to experience true forgiveness, they would need someone without sin who could serve as the bridge of reconciliation between a holy and righteous Creator and a sinful and rebellious creation. This is exactly what Jesus was able to accomplish. Here are a few verses that describe what has transpired through Jesus' perfect obedience [*my italics below*].

> "Although he was a son, *he learned obedience* through what he suffered."
> Hebrews 5:8

> "For we do not have a high priest [Christ] who is unable to sympathize with our weaknesses, but one who in every respect has been tempted as we are, *yet without sin*."
> Hebrews 4:15

> "*He committed no sin*, neither was deceit found in his mouth."
> 1 Peter 2:22

> "You know that he appeared in order to take away sins, and *in him there is no sin*."
> 1 John 3:5

It was imperative that Jesus be born, live and die as an individual who had never sinned, for only a guiltless person would possess the sufficient credentials to approach a holy God and submit the required payment for guilty men and women to be forgiven of their sin, which leads us to our next truth about the historical Jesus.

Fact #3 About Jesus - Although innocent of any crime or wrongdoing, he was cruelly beaten and hung upon a cross to die

Throughout the Bible we are told that the only method by which sin can be removed is for someone who is qualified to pay the penalty for sin with lifeblood. A willing sacrifice of death must be offered in order to satisfy God's required payment for sin. Death is what we all deserve, but this exacting of payment is what Jesus, the Innocent, fully accomplished on our behalf. In fact, this was his primary focal point for coming into this world. This is why he had to become the Infinite God-Man; this is why he had to remain obedient without sinning, so he could be fully approved to offer his own sinless life in exchange for the debt of sin we owed. Without his sacrificial death on our behalf, we are a people without any hope.

This act was the most marvelous expression of unconditional love ever placed on display, an innocent man giving his life for those who were either unaware of his existence or perhaps knew something about him but did not want anything to do with him. And in spite of our continued rejection of him, God's love has never changed, it just keeps on coming.

> "But God shows his love for us in that while we were still sinners, Christ died for us."
>
> Romans 5:8

> "For our sake he made him to be sin who knew no sin, so that in him we might become the righteousness of God."
>
> 2 Corinthians 5:21

> "For God so loved the world, that he gave his only Son, that whoever believes in him should not perish but have eternal life."
>
> John 3:16

Jesus had every right to be declared innocent and to command the heavenly host of angels to come and rescue him, yet he quietly and humbly submitted himself to suffering and rejection of men and women. After being beaten beyond recognition, he was unjustly sentenced to a criminal's death on a cross. His death became the 'payment in full' for our sin. Jesus voluntarily laid down his own life for our sake so that we could experience complete forgiveness of sin and be reconciled to our God.

Question, how can we be sure that this is what the death of Christ really accomplished? We find the answers in the fourth truth about Jesus.

Fact #4 About Jesus - On the third day after his death, he was raised supernaturally from the dead

I can't begin to imagine what it must have felt like to closely follow the man, Jesus, to watch him live his life without slipping up a single time in word, thought and deed, and then to witness him be unjustly killed by his enemies just three years into his mission. Jesus was a relatively young man, probably in his early 30's when he died. I, for one, would have had an awful lot of questions and even more doubts. That is exactly what we witness in the biblical record regarding his followers. Withdrawing from Jesus and now in hiding, fearing for their own lives only hours after his burial, they seem to have become nothing more than a makeshift band of leaderless misfits. But three days after his tragic death something would happen so dramatic that it would change not only the lives of his followers, but also the entire course of history. On Sunday morning some 2,000 years ago, Jesus, the Christ, rose bodily from the dead.

The resurrection of Jesus is one of the most hotly contested events in history. Yet there is plenty of evidence supporting it. Here are a few biblical references regarding the historicity of the resurrection of Jesus.

- **Roman soldiers did in fact confirm Jesus was dead.**

> "But when they [the Roman soldiers] came to Jesus and saw that he was already dead, they did not break his legs. But one of the soldiers pierced his side with a spear, and at once there came out blood and water."
>
> John 19:33-34

- **He was buried in a tomb, which the Roman soldiers sealed and guarded.**

   "Therefore order the tomb to be made secure until the third day, lest his disciples go and steal him away and tell the people, 'He has risen from the dead,' and the last fraud will be worse than the first." Pilate said to them, "You have a guard of soldiers. Go, make it as secure as you can." So they went and made the tomb secure by sealing the stone and setting a guard."

   Matthew 27:64-66

- **The morning of his resurrection visible proof was offered that Jesus did in fact rise from the dead.**

   "Now after the Sabbath, toward the dawn of the first day of the week, Mary Magdalene and the other Mary went to see the tomb. And behold, there was a great earthquake, for an angel of the Lord descended from heaven and came and rolled back the stone and sat on it. His appearance was like lightning, and his clothing white as snow. And for fear of him the guards trembled and became like dead men. But the angel said to the women, "Do not be afraid, for I know that you seek Jesus who was crucified. He is not here, for he has risen, as he said. Come, see the place where he lay.""

Matthew 28:1-6

"While they were perplexed about this, behold, two men stood by them in dazzling apparel. And as they were frightened and bowed their faces to the ground, the men said to them, "Why do you seek the living among the dead? He is not here, but has risen.""

Luke 24:4-6

- **Jesus was seen by over 500 people who testified he had been raised from the dead.**

"He presented himself alive to them after his suffering by many proofs, appearing to them during forty days and speaking about the kingdom of God."

Acts 1:3

"As they were talking about these things, Jesus himself stood among them, and said to them, "Peace to you!" But they were startled and frightened and thought they saw a spirit. And he said to them, "Why are you troubled, and why do doubts arise in your hearts? See my hands and my feet, that it is I myself. Touch me, and see. For a spirit does not have flesh and bones as you see that I have." And when he had said this, he showed them his hands and his feet."

Luke 24:36-40

"For I delivered to you as of first importance what I also received: that Christ died for our sins in accordance with the Scriptures, that he was buried, that he was raised on the third day in accordance with the Scriptures, and that he appeared to Cephas, then to the twelve. Then he appeared to more than five hundred brothers at one time, most of whom are still alive, though some have fallen asleep. Then he appeared to James, then to all the apostles. Last of all, as to one untimely born, he appeared also to me."

1 Corinthians 15:3-8

- **Jesus in his resurrected body openly demonstrated before others his divine power over everything.**

One question we have yet to ask ourselves, *Why is the resurrection a necessary component in God's story of salvation?* The resurrection of Jesus is our proof that the work of Christ on the cross was indeed effectual and eternal life a reality. The apostle Paul puts it this way [*my italics below*]:

> "Now if Christ is proclaimed as raised from the dead, how can some of you say that there is no resurrection of the dead? But if there is no resurrection of the dead, then not even Christ has been raised. And if Christ has not been raised, then our preaching is in vain and your faith is in vain. We are even found to be misrepresenting God, because we testified about God that he raised Christ, whom he did not raise if it is true that the dead are not raised. For if the dead are not raised, not even Christ has been raised. And *if Christ has not been raised, your faith is futile and you are still in your sins.*"
>
> 1 Corinthians 15:12-17

In other words, if there is no resurrection, there is no payment for sin and thus there is no eternal life. Jesus' death on the cross would have been considered pointless and in vain without the resurrection. Christ is now considered the first born among his brothers. He was raised in power, demonstrating that he had all authority over death and hell. The stinging power of death's finality no longer held sway over Jesus and those he calls his brothers and sisters.

Are you beginning to understand the great lengths God was willing to go in order to be able to extend complete forgiveness of sins and grant eternal life to anyone who would say an authentic, "Yes," to him? The resurrection is the ultimate display of God's sovereign power over all of creation, including death. And it was after the resurrection that Jesus began to share his powers of discernment and impart courage with his disciples. Look at Luke's description of the disciples' encounter with Jesus as they hid themselves [*my italics below*].

> "As they were talking about these things, Jesus himself stood among them, and said to them, "Peace to you!"

> But they were startled and frightened and thought they saw a spirit. And he said to them, "Why are you troubled, and why do doubts arise in your hearts? See my hands and my feet, that it is I myself. Touch me, and see. For a spirit does not have flesh and bones as you see that I have." And when he had said this, he showed them his hands and his feet. And while they still disbelieved for joy and were marveling, he said to them, "Have you anything here to eat?" They gave him a piece of broiled fish, and he took it and ate before them. *Then he opened their minds to understand the Scriptures, and said to them, "Thus it is written, that the Christ should suffer and on the third day rise from the dead, and that repentance and forgiveness of sins should be proclaimed in his name to all nations.""*
>
> Luke 24:36-47

From this point forward the disciples no longer were overcome with fear of what might happen to them. Jesus, in his resurrected state, extended to his followers power and understanding of why everything had to happen the way it did. For the first time in their short three years with him they were able to connect the dots of God's grand plan of salvation. But the story does not end here. Let's consider another aspect of the life of Jesus in his post-resurrection body.

Fact #5 About Jesus - Forty days after his resurrection, he visibly ascended into heaven

We read previously that Jesus appeared to hundreds of people during the forty-day period after his resurrection. What happened next historically is yet another demonstration of God's unlimited abilities and perfect plan to look after and save his people. You recall that the title for Jesus is, 'the Christ.' This title means that he has been granted the titles of Prophet, Priest and King over his people. Late in his ministry Jesus began alerting his disciples that he was going to have to go away, but he told them not to worry, for he would send a Comforter to them, namely, the Holy Spirit. They didn't understand at first, but with this newfound post-resurrection insight, they could begin to see beyond what their physical eyes could tell them. Listen to Luke's description of what actually happened at what is known as the ascension of Jesus, the Christ.

> "So when they had come together, they asked him, "Lord, will you at this time restore the kingdom to Israel?" He said to them, "It is not for you to know times or seasons that the Father has fixed by his own authority. But you will receive power when the Holy Spirit has come upon you, and you will be my witnesses in Jerusalem and in all Judea and Samaria, and to the end of the earth." And when he had said these things, as they were looking on, he was lifted up, and a cloud took him out of their sight."
>
> Acts 1:6-9

What in fact was happening is that Jesus was ascending back to the place from whence he came. He rightfully took his seat once again at the right hand of Father and began to function as our perfect Prophet, Priest and King. As our Prophet, he provides communication of truth from God and what his will is for our lives. As our Priest, he lives to intercede (pray) for us. As our King, he reigns over us as a flawless ruler, full of compassion, mercy and justice.

So, you may ask, if this is where Jesus ended up, and he is still there functioning in these three roles, what is next on God's agenda? We will now address the sixth and final fact about Jesus, for it is in understanding this truth one can perhaps begin to understand the motive for a book such as this.

Fact #6 About Jesus - He promises that he will return one day soon to judge the living and the dead

The second coming of Jesus could be described as the culmination of God's wonderful plan to save his people for all eternity. God, in his infinite understanding and foreknowledge, knew that in order to get us from point A to point B—to the place of being able to receive the gift of eternal life—he would have to orchestrate a plan that by human standards, would seem quite unorthodox. Yet, in God's scheme of things it makes perfect sense. This is why he is God… and we are not. His working, his methods, his decisions are always bound in perfect, yet often undisclosed wisdom.

God's control over all things will be demonstrated once again in the visible return of Jesus, the Christ. As his followers, we have been instructed to not concern ourselves with trying to figure out the exact time of his return, because only God knows when it will happen. Yes, a lot of well-meaning people have speculated, but they continuously miss the mark, revealing once again that this whole plan is a God thing and not a man thing. Here are a few verses that assure us of the reality that when Christ does return it will be an event that will be witnessed by all.

> "So Christ, having been offered once to bear the sins of many, will appear a second time, not to deal with sin but to save those who are eagerly waiting for him."
>
> Hebrews 9:28

> "Behold, he is coming with the clouds, and every eye will see him, even those who pierced him, and all tribes of the earth will wail on account of him. Even so. Amen."
>
> Revelation 1:7

"When Christ who is your life appears, then you also will appear with him in glory."
$$\text{Colossians 3:4}$$

"For as the lightning comes from the east and shines as far as the west, so will be the coming of the Son of Man."
$$\text{Matthew 24:27}$$

"Therefore you also must be ready, for the Son of Man is coming at an hour you do not expect."
$$\text{Matthew 24:44}$$

Do you see the two common threads running through these few selected verses?

1. Christ will visibly return for all to see.
2. We are told to be eagerly expecting his return.

Please consider this; God, your Creator, has a timetable from which he will initiate the final act of mankind. Once the clock strikes at the appointed time, it will be too late for those who have chosen to not repent. This is why you are encouraged to repent now and not later. God, your Creator, has initiated the opportunity to have a relationship with you. He's made a way for you to experience forgiveness of all sin and wrongdoing. He has accomplished the impossible, because with God, all things are possible. Consider these two pivotal verses:

> "For he [God] says,
> "In a favorable time I listened to you,
>   and in a day of salvation I have
> helped you."
> Behold, now is the favorable time;
> behold, now is the day of salvation."
>
> 2 Corinthians 6:2

> "But what does it say? "The word is near you, in your mouth and in your heart" (that is, the word of faith that we proclaim); because, if you confess with your mouth that Jesus is Lord and believe in your heart that God raised him from the dead, you will be saved. For with the heart one believes and is justified, and with the mouth one confesses and is saved. For the Scripture says, "Everyone who believes in him will not be put to shame.""
>
> Romans 10:8-11

As we have seen, reconciliation is an essential ingredient to repentance because it involves believing in and actually accepting the finished work of Jesus, the Christ. Without Jesus, we cannot be restored to a right relationship with God. I hope you can begin to see how critical it is that this ingredient be added at just the right time for one to experience true and authentic repentance. That said, we dare not deemphasize the fourth and final ingredient, for without this fourth ingredient, the three previous ingredients will never have their intended effect on a person.

13.
The Fourth Ingredient: Redirection

Several decades ago I partnered with a prison ministry organization in the Midwest visiting local and county jails, state and federal penitentiaries, halfway houses, etc., sharing what God had done in my own life. It was intriguing to note there were two themes commonly shared by nearly every inmate I met: 1. They were always innocent. 2. They promised that if they ever got out of jail they would never commit a crime again. Unfortunately, as we have learned the truth about the plight of the human condition, apart from God it is impossible to keep our promises of never doing wrong. The reason for this? Because no one starts out as truly innocent. Every inmate I encountered was there because they had been declared guilty, based on the evidence of the crime in question. Still, there were always some inmates who, in spite of their guilt, tried to circumvent the system by suddenly getting 'jailhouse religion,' playing the game of trying to do good in front of others in order to perhaps obtain favor and an early release. Not being genuine, it is only a matter of time before it will become obvious to all around them that this new lease on life was in fact not a real change of life at all.

As any inmate will tell you, evidence in a case is critical. In the same manner, God's economy depends upon the effective use of evidence. Evidence will either work for you or it will work against you. I, in this case, want it to work for you. This is where our fourth and final ingredient is added and the recipe begins to take shape. *Redirection* is what completes true repentance. God tells us that if we have responded properly out of soul-stirring conviction, if we have confessed our sins and placed our hope in him, and if we have been truly reconciled with him through the finished work of his Son, Jesus, there is always going to be indisputable evidence that what we have experienced is indeed genuine. In the same fashion, if our decision to change is not genuine (e.g., jailhouse religion), that will eventually become apparent to all as well. So again, evidence can work for you or it can work against you.

Did you know the word repentance in its most basic sense means to have a change of mind? But to get at the fuller expression of the word we need to grasp what this 'change of mind' entails. When we refer to the mind in this way, we are talking about the entire inner being of a person. Repentance is more than just a mental ascent or agreement with someone or something. Here's a truth that will help you get a better handle on the word, authentic repentance always begins with the internal thoughts of a person and migrates to the external actions of a person. In other words, a change of mind always results in a change of action. True repentance will begin to become evident before others as we begin to live this new life from the inside out. This is exactly the evidence God is looking for in a person who repents. Some have also described the concept of change in the word repentance as a 180° turn in life, meaning a person who changes direction who is say, headed north, and suddenly does an about face turning away from where he or she was going and begins to head south. Bottom-line, it is important that you understand that repentance means 'to change.' This happens supernaturally when we've responded, through true conviction, by confessing our sins and receiving in faith the forgiveness of God through the work of his Son, Jesus and thus reconciled in relationship with him. It is all because of this that we want to begin living differently. In its fullest sense, this is what it means to have a change of mind.

So, what is the evidence one should expect to see in their life that would affirm that their repentance and experience with God is authentic and ongoing? Let me offer three pieces of evidence that will always reside in a person who has been truly changed:

1. A repentant person will begin to think differently

While those around us may not be able to hear our inner-thoughts, God always does. He reminds us that he never sleeps nor slumbers. He is aware at all times. Jesus reminded us that the words that come out of our mouth reveal what is in the heart and the mind. When we repent we are agreeing to step onto the path of transformation and allow the Spirit of God to teach us how we should think differently. Read over these verses regarding the thinking process for the follower of God.

Is God Real and Does It Even Matter?

"I appeal to you therefore, brothers, by the mercies of God, to present your bodies as a living sacrifice, holy and acceptable to God, which is your spiritual worship. Do not be conformed to this world, but be transformed by the renewal of your mind, that by testing you may discern what is the will of God, what is good and acceptable and perfect."
Romans 12:1-2

"Finally, brothers, whatever is true, whatever is honorable, whatever is just, whatever is pure, whatever is lovely, whatever is commendable, if there is any excellence, if there is anything worthy of praise, think about these things."
Philippians 4:8

"Set your minds on things that are above, not on things that are on earth."
Colossians 3:2

"So we do not lose heart. Though our outer self is wasting away, our inner self is being renewed day by day."
2 Corinthians 4:16

> "Have this mind among yourselves, which is yours in Christ Jesus."
>
> Philippians 2:5

Success in changing our thinking is the first piece of evidence you can evaluate and know that your repentance is genuine. While we may not always succeed at thinking the right thing at any given moment, for the person in true relationship with God there will always be an awareness of the need to think rightly and a concerted effort to do so. The mere desire to move forward in your thinking, to take on the mind of Christ, is confirmation that repentance is real. And the fact is that a person in true repentance will have more and more success in right thinking as they continue with God in relationship. The power of God within you is there to enable you to change the way you think. It is important to remember that this process of learning to think rightly never stops on this side of eternity. As his sons and daughters, we are always in the throes of learning how to change our thinking and to think rightly in all circumstances. That is part of our growing up in him.

2. A repentant person will begin to speak differently

In this day and age where obscenity seems to have become an acceptable form of communication even by many who profess to be a follower of Jesus, it can prove challenging for a Christian to develop a different vocabulary. We are seeing this more and more as social media dominates our daily routine. But speech full of vulgarity, gossip and condemnation—even behind the keyboard—by men and women who claim to know God, actually devalues his transformative nature in their lives. As a new follower of Jesus, it is imperative that a person be made aware that the Spirit of God within them intends to affect every aspect of their life, including control of the tongue. What we say and how we say it matters a lot to God. It is a sign we are under the control of the Spirit of God. A change in how we converse will be a significant signpost that repentance is having its intended effect on our lives. Listen carefully to the words of these verses:

> "Let no corrupting talk come out of
> your mouths, but only such as is good
> for building up, as fits the occasion,

that it may give grace to those who hear."

> Ephesians 4:29

"Let there be no filthiness nor foolish talk nor crude joking, which are out of place, but instead let there be thanksgiving."

> Ephesians 5:4

"But now you must put them all away: anger, wrath, malice, slander, and obscene talk from your mouth. Do not lie to one another, seeing that you have put off the old self with its practices and have put on the new self, which is being renewed in knowledge after the image of its creator."

> Colossians 3:8-10

"Let your speech always be gracious, seasoned with salt, so that you may know how you ought to answer each person."

> Colossians 4:6

We must be aware that once words, good or bad, are spoken, we can never retrieve them. They are forever cast into the air for all listening to collect, translate and apply. This is why we are encouraged to always be careful how we speak, and when we do we speak as 'seasoned with salt,' casting flavor into the atmosphere rather than creating an ugly distaste for conversation. Again, our speech, like our thinking, is something that can only be tamed and transformed by the Spirit of God within us once we repent.

A repentant person is willing to be completely transformed by the power of God, no matter what it may require. Yes, it is possible, even in this culture, for a Christian to speak differently. A repentant person will not conform to the vocabulary of this world. He or she is able to speak new and fresh words, phrases and sentences that will bring honor to God.

Let's move now to the third piece of evidence when true repentance is present.

3. A repentant person will begin to act differently

It is essential that we take what we know about God and his commands and put them into practice in everyday living. To let this entire reading exercise become merely a reservoir for expanding knowledge misses the point of the book entirely. What we are talking about is the complete transformation of a person from the inside out. You cannot escape the fact that what a person does directly reflects how he or she thinks. If we think improperly our behavior will reflect that in wrong choices because choices are always based on what we think. This is why it is so important that we first concentrate on letting God change our thinking, which then will affect our doing. What we do and how we treat others will be the telltale sign of what's really going on inside us. Listen to these declarations regarding the importance of always striving to do good, which begins with right thinking.

> "And whatever you do, in word or deed, do everything in the name of the Lord Jesus."
>
> Colossians 3:17

> "And let us not grow weary of doing good, for in due season we will reap, if we do not give up."
>
> Galatians 6:9

> "See that no one repays anyone evil for evil, but always seek to do good to one another and to everyone."
>
> 1 Thessalonians 5:15

> "Love is patient and kind; love does not envy or boast; it is not arrogant or rude. It does not insist on its own way; it is not irritable or resentful; it does not rejoice at wrongdoing, but rejoices with the truth. Love bears all things, believes all things, hopes all things, endures all things."
>
> 1 Corinthians 13:4-7

The presence of these three evidentiary pieces can help serve as a personal litmus test for authentic repentance. But it is important to note that when I say personal, I don't mean we are the ones who have the final say in our lives. If we are God's in relationship, we must ask him to reveal to us our present condition. We must ask his Spirit to search us and see if there are any ungodly ways in us. If there are, we must ask for help in correcting any thoughts, words or deeds out of sync with his will for us. And as we confess we are sorry for what we have thought, said or done we must also be willing to accept his complete forgiveness in the same way a son or daughter would receive forgiveness from a parent and move forward in the relationship. If we as children found ourselves only able to utter, "I'm sorry, I'm sorry, I'm sorry," what type of family dynamic would that be? I know as a parent if that were all I heard from my son or daughter, I would quickly reason that my child has yet to learn how to live in a healthy familial relationship. It is the same way with God. No doubt he wants us to repent, but he also wants us to get beyond the perpetual 'I'm sorry'. We learn that by accepting in faith what Jesus has done on our behalf.

What Jesus accomplished in his life, death and resurrection he did so that we could have life, and experience it in abundance. This does not mean that an abundance of things is to be expected, but that our relationship with him would be full of life. God promises that in Christ our time here on earth can be so much more than just existing in the mundane, trudging through just trying to get by. Although it doesn't mean the days will necessarily get easier or the nights get quieter, it does mean that the one with whom you have relationship will be there in every situation to give hope, meaning and purpose and to help you keep an eye to the bigger picture of eternity. Life in Christ promises to be full of the good things God has promised, peace of mind, joy in the soul and the confidence to accomplish anything he asks you to do. He will give you a new power to love where you've been unwilling to love, to forgive where you've been unwilling to forgive, and to go where you've been unwilling to go, and to do it with the satisfaction knowing that you have been given everything you need. But in order to get to that place with Jesus, where we have that type of life, we have to first admit that we have, in essence, been dead in our sin and therefore unresponsive to the things of God... until now. According to the truth of the Bible, once true repentance happens, all things change. All things are made new. When we humbly repent and accept what Jesus has done on our behalf, we are privy to receive the ultimate 'do over' in life. If you are ready for this to happen in your life, then by all means, please read on.

14.
I Once Was Blind but Now I See

You recall a few pages back our introduction of a new character, Jesus, in the cast of God's story? It is time to introduce one more character. *Enter Holy Spirit stage above.* You recall in an earlier verse depicting the ascension of Jesus where after forty days he was taken up into heaven to take his reserved seat at the right hand of God? The account is recorded in the book of Acts. Note there was a particular statement Jesus made during his departure that we will now focus upon [*my italics below*].

> "So when they had come together, they asked him, "Lord, will you at this time restore the kingdom to Israel?" He said to them, "It is not for you to know times or seasons that the Father has fixed by his own authority. *But you will receive power when the Holy Spirit has come upon you,* and you will be my

witnesses in Jerusalem and in all Judea and Samaria, and to the end of the earth." And when he had said these things, as they were looking on, he was lifted up, and a cloud took him out of their sight."

Acts 1:6-9

Notice it says, *"But you will receive power when the Holy Spirit has come upon you."* The wonderful aspect to the story of God is that he has promised to never leave us to fend for ourselves in this world that is often hostile toward Jesus and those who claim to follow him. We, along with his disciples left standing staring into the sky, have the promise that the Holy Spirit will come to dwell within, to guide, comfort and empower us. Let's examine a few passages of Scripture that illuminate the purpose of the Holy Spirit's presence in our lives.

The Holy Spirit Guides:

> "When the Spirit of truth comes, he will guide you into all the truth, for he will not speak on his own authority, but whatever he hears he will speak, and

he will declare to you the things that are to come."
> John 16:13

"Now we have received not the spirit of the world, but the Spirit who is from God, that we might understand the things freely given us by God. And we impart this in words not taught by human wisdom but taught by the Spirit, interpreting spiritual truths to those who are spiritual."
> 1 Corinthians 2:12-13

The Holy Spirit Comforts:

"Nevertheless, I tell you the truth: it is to your advantage that I go away, for if I do not go away, the Helper will not come to you. But if I go, I will send him to you."
> John 16:7

"If you love me [Jesus], you will keep my commandments. And I will ask the Father, and he will give you another Helper, to be with you forever, even the Spirit of truth, whom the world cannot receive, because it neither sees him nor knows him. You know him, for he dwells with you and will be in you."

John 14:15-17

The Holy Spirit Empowers:

"If the Spirit of him who raised Jesus from the dead dwells in you, he who raised Christ Jesus from the dead will also give life to your mortal bodies through his Spirit who dwells in you."

Romans 8:11

"For the grace of God has appeared, bringing salvation for all people, training us to renounce ungodliness and worldly passions, and to live self-controlled, upright, and godly lives in the present age."

Titus 2:11-12

What a wonderful collection of truths about how the Holy Spirit truly aids us in our relationship with God. But did you know the scope of the Spirit's work goes even further than what is described in the verses above? If you are reading this book and you are sensing something you did not expect and you now find yourself wanting to consider what God is offering, I am confident the Holy Spirit is already readily at work in you... and you most likely are not even be aware it is happening. Know this, the Spirit of God is always at work behind the scenes, softening and penetrating hearts that were thought to be calloused and pretty much impenetrable. Here are three truths that explain how the Spirit of God works in a person to make them aware of God and their need for him in their lives.

The Holy Spirit is the only one who gives sight to the spiritually blind:

> "And even if our gospel is veiled, it is veiled to those who are perishing. In their case the god of this world has blinded the minds of the unbelievers, to keep them from seeing the light of the gospel of the glory of Christ, who is the image of God. For what we proclaim is not ourselves, but Jesus Christ as Lord, with ourselves as your servants for Jesus' sake. For God, who said, "Let light shine out of darkness," has shone in our hearts to give the light

of the knowledge of the glory of God in the face of Jesus Christ."
>2 Corinthians 4:3-6

"For at one time you were darkness, but now you are light in the Lord. Walk as children of light."
>Ephesians 5:8

The Holy Spirit is the only one who brings about a sense of conviction in a person:

"Nevertheless, I tell you the truth: it is to your advantage that I go away, for if I do not go away, the Helper will not come to you. But if I go, I will send him to you. And when he comes, he will convict the world concerning sin and righteousness and judgment: concerning sin, because they do not believe in me; concerning righteousness, because I go to the Father, and you will see me no longer; concerning judgment, because the ruler of this world is judged."
>John 16:7-11

The Holy Spirit is the only one who gives us the ability to say, "Yes," to God:

> "And you were dead in the trespasses and sins in which you once walked, following the course of this world, following the prince of the power of the air, the spirit that is now at work in the sons of disobedience—among whom we all once lived in the passions of our flesh, carrying out the desires of the body and the mind, and were by nature children of wrath, like the rest of mankind. But God, being rich in mercy, because of the great love with which he loved us, even when we were dead in our trespasses, made us alive together with Christ—by grace you have been saved—and raised us up with him and seated us with him in the heavenly places in Christ Jesus, so that in the coming ages he might show the immeasurable riches of his grace in kindness toward us in Christ Jesus."
>
> Ephesians 2:1-7

The Bible describes the human condition apart from the Holy Spirit's direct intervention this way: a total preoccupation with self, an inability to choose God on their own because they are spiritually dead, and a spiritual blindness to see the need to accept God's open invitation to experience real life. Without the work of the Holy Spirit to impart sight and life there is no hope for any man or woman. Again, this is where the love of God, in spite of our insistence to love self first, is displayed on every page of the Bible. God's desire is that the reality of this story will jump off the pages right into your heart and become something truly transformative. And he's willing to help make that possible.

15.
What Now?

We've covered a lot of ground. You've got a lot to think about. I hope you'll use this book to go back and reread and ponder as you consider a personal relationship with God. I'm not going to ask that you make an impulsive decision about God, his offer and his place in your life. I will say this, God personally invites you and me to come and reason together. Jesus also tells us to carefully consider the cost of this new life in him. That said, as you ponder these truths, note there will never be a better offer to come your way. God is extending to you a clean slate, a real chance to start over. Yes, there will be things in your past that may never go away. Those are the consequences of the choices we make. But God has promised that in the midst of all of those circumstances he will never leave you nor forsake you as you journey through this life.

Of course, if you are prepared right now to enter into this new and exciting relationship with God, I don't want you to delay for a single moment. It's just that you need to make sure you are ready and willing for the right reasons. Let me ask some basic questions for your consideration. Be honest with yourself:

1. Do you believe in the existence of the one true God as described in the Bible?
2. Do you believe he is the Creator of all things?
3. Do you believe he is your Creator?
4. Do you believe you are personally accountable to him?
5. Do you believe you have sinned against him and deserve his judgment?
6. Do you want to be forgiven of all of your sin and inherit eternal life?
7. Do you believe that Jesus, the Christ, in his obedience, death and resurrection paid the price for your sin?
8. Do you want to reach out in faith and receive what God is offering you through his Son?
9. Are you willing to confess with your mouth that Jesus is Lord and believe in your heart that God has raised him from the dead?

If the answer is yes, know that the Spirit of God has opened your eyes to see the truth and is enabling you to believe in the work Jesus has done on your behalf. I encourage you, right now, stop reading and tell God audibly what is on your heart. Ask him for help to understand what it is he is asking you to do and remind him that he has promised to help you by giving you the Spirit so you can have the power to walk into a new life in him.

Talk to him now; confess your sins, receive his remedy for being reconciled, accept the work of salvation that his Son completed on your behalf, and then begin to live a life of redirection.

Mind you, he, being God, already knows what's on your heart, but like a parent who is aware of what their child has done, a father knows the good it will do for the child to come forward, confess, come clean and receive forgiveness. God has been patiently waiting to hear from you and receive you as a son or daughter.

The Christian life can be experienced in such a vast array of expressions. I don't have a particular formula to put forth on what should happen now. You may have a sense of feeling washed and sparkling clean. You may be ecstatic and finding it difficult to put into words. You may want to immediately tell someone, perhaps a close friend or family member who has been praying for you. You may not feel much at all. It is important to remember that your feelings, while important to you, cannot be the determining factor in what you decide to do and not do. What God is asking of each of us is a decision based upon faith in him and what we believe to be true based upon the story he has told us in the Bible. If you've decided to accept God's offer of forgiveness and eternal life, then trust him that this is what has happened. Listen to this truth found in 1 John.

> "I write these things to you who
> believe in the name of the Son of God,
> that you may know that you have
> eternal life."
>
> 1 John 5:13

Do you see what this verse is declaring? It is telling you that the Bible's story is true... so true that you can have absolute confidence that what it promises regarding eternal life through Jesus was indeed accomplished and will come to pass. Jesus did what you and I could not do on our own. And all this comes to each of us as a free gift from God, his idea, his plan, his implementation and his seeing it through to the end.

16.
It's Your Move

If you are still on the fence regarding this invitation or have even jumped off to the other side and have chosen not to accept the reliability of the Bible's story, I encourage you to keep pursuing the truth about the existence of God. Ask God to make himself known to you, to open your eyes and reveal to you if these truths are authentic or not. I am confident God will honor your seeking him.

Do remember this, to refrain from making the choice to accept God's offer is in fact a 'no' decision. In God's economy, there is no such word as 'maybe,' or phrase, 'perhaps one day.' Again, your indecision will be treated as a 'no' decision by God. Can you make a decision later? Sure. But as we all know, we have no guarantees we will be here tomorrow, or even in the next minute. That is why the invitation is to accept him today. Nonetheless, if you are unsure or unwilling, I don't want to be guilty of forcing your hand to do something that would be half-hearted or less than authentic. I encourage you in your pursuits to be fully convinced one way or the other and then live consistently with your convictions.

If you have said 'Yes,' to God's invitation for forgiveness and eternal life, that is wonderful. I would encourage you to do the following as you begin your new journey in Christ:

1. Talk and listen to God regularly. Tell him what's on your mind. Don't hide doubts and misgivings. He wants to hear everything so he can establish relationship and build your confidence that he does indeed answer prayer. Don't forget to take some time to listen to what he is saying to you as well. If we quieten ourselves, he will make himself known. Remember, God is big and already knows what is going on. Our talking and listening to him is primarily for our benefit and growth as a Christian.

2. Ask God for the Spirit regularly. We need the Spirit's presence in our lives for direction, power and discernment. We also want the Spirit in our lives because we are in relationship with God. The Spirit can reveal to us things we need to know, both about God and about life, and gives us the ability to accomplish what God asks us to do. Christians are encouraged to regularly be filled with the Spirit. We do this because the Spirit is our source for living life victoriously.

3. Read the Bible regularly. The Bible is God's story written for our benefit. When we read the Bible, we get to know the heart of God and why he does what he does. Where should you begin as a new follower of Christ? I would suggest either the book of John or the book of Luke. As you grow in Christ you'll need to avoid reading the Bible selectively. Read all of it instead, knowing that in both the plain and simple truths as well as the deep reservoirs of wisdom, God is there on every page.

4. Find a church that promotes a high view of God, Jesus, the Holy Spirit, Water Baptism and the Bible. Unfortunately, we've got to exercise some care in this area. Not every church is the same. Do some investigating before you jump in. Get advice from other trusted Christians if you are unsure. Once you do locate a healthy body of believers, get involved and become a part of God's family.

You might want to read over the book of Acts to get an idea of how the first century Christians did church together.

5. Expect change to come. If the Spirit of God is dwelling in you it is inevitable that you are going to begin seeing things differently. This is called the fruit of repentance. The change that will come into your life, how you think, speak and act will become evident to you and those around you. Here is a verse that will help you understand that this work in you is truly a supernatural work of the Spirit.

> "But the fruit of the Spirit is love, joy, peace, patience, kindness, goodness, faithfulness, gentleness, self-control."
> Galatians 5:22-23

SPECIAL NOTE: When we begin to experience real change within, it can be quite exciting. Naturally we will want others, those we love and care about, to experience the same thing we've just walked through. In your fervor, I encourage you to resist the temptation to coerce another to change for change's sake, or to judge them because they are not interested in what you are offering. Remember, God's timing is perfect. Let him use you to gently influence the person you care about and begin praying that the Spirit of God would open his or her eyes just as he opened yours. You'll be amazed at how God will work his story into their lives.

Final Thoughts

No matter where you are on the one true God spectrum, yes, no, or maybe, I want to personally thank you for giving this book consideration. Your time is valuable and I want you to use it wisely. I hope you feel the read has been worthwhile, whether you agree or not. And while there is a lot more to the story, I feel I have provided you enough material to get you started on your own journey. It is my hope that you will consider this a starting place to begin seeking the one true God of the Bible, for only in him is forgiveness and life eternal.

> "And without faith it is impossible to please him, for whoever would draw near to God must believe that he exists and that he rewards those who seek him."
>
> Hebrews 11:6

If you would like to place a copy of this book into the hands of an acquaintance, colleague, friend and/or family member, ask for it at your favorite local book store or you can order it online @ www.lightchaserpress.com. Note volume purchase discounts are also available.

Rick would like to hear from you.

Rick Furmanek
c/o Light Chaser Press
PO Box 2194
Gilbert, AZ 85299

or

You may use the comment section on the contact page on our website @ www.lightchaserpress.com/contact.html

www.ingramcontent.com/pod-product-compliance
Lightning Source LLC
Chambersburg PA
CBHW052026290426
44112CB00014B/2393